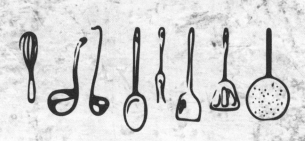

Cold-pressed Beverages

Health and Well-being in a Glass

WHITE STAR PUBLISHERS

Photographs and Recipes
CINZIA TRENCHI

Project Editor
VALERIA MANFERTO DE FABIANIS

Graphic Layout
VALENTINA GIAMMARINARO

INTRODUCTION

Recipes

PREPARATIONS WITH CEREALS, NUTS AND LEGUMES

THE AUTHOR

Introduction

Unlike any other preparations, slow-pressed juices are a nutritional resource that can complete a healthy, balanced diet, supplying minerals, vitamins and fiber extracted from a variety of foods ranging from cereals to nuts, fruits and vegetables.

Cold-pressed juices differ from a smoothie, are more well-rounded than a regular juice and more nutritious than centrifugally-extracted juices. They can be easily prepared using a masticating juicer: a household appliance that does not alter the active compounds contained in foods. As a result, the preparation retains most of the nutrients of the chosen ingredients.

These beverages are recommended for people who lead busy lives, are athletically active or who are searching for a way to eat healthy but don't have a lot of time to dedicate to cooking. They are a way to pamper, pamper and detoxify the body, lower calorie intake or simply to transform fruits and vegetables into attractive and tasty preparations to entice someone who has little appetite or who would like to substitute a traditional meal with a simple beverage.

The consistency of a beverage prepared in a masticating juicer can be fluffy, creamy and velvety or fluid like water; it can be diluted with ice, transformed into a sorbet, mixed with cereal milks or substituted for lunch or dinner.

The masticating juicer is the next step in the evolution of traditional systems such as the blender and the centrifugal juicer; thanks to its mechanical characteristics, in addition to preparing tasty juices, it ensures the retention of almost all of the beneficial characteristics of foods, which are often lost during other preparation methods. A cold-pressed juice can be thought of as a healthier version of that ideal juice suitable to any diet or age-group: for children, expectant mothers and the elderly. When purchasing the appliance, several very important factors must be taken into consideration: the price, which can vary from 50 to 1,000 dollars; and the technical characteristics (the lower the rpm, the more food characteristics are preserved, because they are exposed to less heat). Even the filters supplied are important: fine mesh filters are great for juices, while those with a coarser mesh are needed for denser preparations. In some cases, this home appliance also includes accessories for preparing sorbets and sauces.

However, the fundamental question is "which foods should be used to prepare cold-pressed juices?" All fruits are welcome: those with high water contents such as watermelon, melon, peaches and oranges, as well as those with little water, such as bananas and avocado. Even nuts (hazelnuts, walnuts, almonds, and pistachios) and seed-rich fruit (blackberries and kiwis) can be used.

When it comes to vegetables, anything you choose will be suitable, including leafy vegetables and herbs, inflorescences such as cauliflower, and of course tomatoes, radishes, cucumbers and anything else you can find at a farmer's market! The only advice to heed is to always use products that are in season because they have the most nutrients.

While the use of fruits and vegetables in preparations is standard practice, the use of cereals, legumes and seeds in home-made beverages is a rather novel idea. Delicious almond, hazelnut, oat or rice based beverages are easy to prepare. Just make sure to follow a few simple suggestions.

For example, nuts should be soaked overnight before use and cereals need to be cooked. Hence, a small time investment and the desire to experiment can transform different nuts and seeds into delicious preparations that are just as excellent as those sold at health stores. You will be able to prepare velvety oat, barley, hazelnut and almond creams, with densities that vary depending on the filter employed, which can be used to enrich fruit and vegetable juices or even combined and used to substitute a meal. Lightness, simplicity and ease of preparation are the goals of recipes for healthy cold-pressed beverages perfect for breakfast or a snack.

Naturally-sweet fruit juices, flavorful vegetable mixes, extravagant spiced or seasoned beverages perfect for cocktails. A preparation of peaches, cocoa powder and hazelnuts can become a delicious dessert that helps keep calories in check and can be transformed into an ice cream; while the pairing of green tea with rice and almond cream can become a summer breakfast that is rich, nutritious and light.

For a hot summer day, a thirst-quenching appointment with a watermelon and cucumber beverage will help you rehydrate without assuming too many calories; while a tomato preparation with thyme and oregano can make an excellent cocktail that is also fantastic served frozen! If on the other hand, you need a beverage that supplies a boost of energy, helps recharge or get through a stressful situation, combine pears, oranges and ginger.

This volume is divided into four chapters that propose fruit-based beverages, beverages with fruits and vegetables, beverages with just vegetables and finally, cereal-based beverages with fruits, vegetables and nuts.

All of the chapters contain simple, healthy recipes for enriching a diet and getting more comfortable with a new way of eating that underscores the importance of using what nature has to offer with care and awareness, in order to enjoy (and hopefully maintain) a feeling of wellbeing!

The watermelon is a fruit of the annual *Citrullus vulgaris* and *Citrullus lanatus* plants, which belong to the Gourd family. It ripens in the summer and is extremely thirst-quenching (containing over 95% water), low in calories (just 15 per 100 g) and rich in potassium, calcium, phosphorus and vitamins including retinol and vitamin C. Finally, it must be noted that it contains lycopene, which has antioxidant properties. It is diuretic, suitable to being consumed cold or cool in fruit salads, juices, smoothies and sorbets. It spoils easily hence it is best to finish it once cut.

WATERMELON

Apricots, a fruit of the *Prunus armeniaca*, contain high quantities of retinol (especially when dried), vitamin C and potassium. They are very useful to athletes (thanks to their potassium content) and to lovers of a good tan, because they facilitate it! Apricots are low in calories (28 per every 100 g). Their pulp is dense, contains 85% water and lends itself to the preparation of velvety smoothies with creamy textures. In addition, apricots are mildly laxative thanks to the presence of sorbitol.

APRICOT

Pineapples contain bromelain, which promotes weight loss. This fruit is thirst-quenching and gives a pleasant feeling of freshness; it combats inflammation and aids protein digestion. It is composed of about 85% water, has few calories (40 per 100 g) and is rich in minerals including potassium, calcium, phosphorus and vitamins A and C. The fruit can be stored for long periods however, to make sure it is fresh before purchasing, check that the leaves are green and fresh-looking and that the aroma is perceptible. To make sure the aroma does not lose its potency, store it outside the fridge.

PINEAPPLE

Asparagus, a must in the kitchens in the spring, is an important anti-inflammatory and diuretic agent. It also aids weight loss by promoting the elimination of excess fluids. Its shoot (the edible portion of the plant) is low in calories (29 per every 100 g) and contains a lot of water (about 91%). It is rich in minerals (calcium, iron and phosphorus) and vitamins (folic acid, C and E). Its juice is refreshing and thirst-quenching, and can make a tasty and healthy cocktail substitute.

ASPARAGUS

ORANGE

The orange is very thirst-quenching
and juicy. The orange tree grows
in mild climates and its fruit,
available from winter to spring,
are energizing and stimulating
to the appetite. In addition,
thanks to their high
vitamin C contents,
eating oranges helps
prevent the common
cold, facilitates
the assimilation
of iron and helps
combat the ageing
of tissues. They
have 34 calories per
100 g, and contain
potassium, which
is particularly
important to
athletes and the
elderly.

Extremely high in protein,
oats are rich in fiber and
particularly helpful in
controlling cholesterol
levels. They contain a
good percentage of lipids,
an excellent amount of
fiber (about 10%!), and many
minerals (such as iron,
calcium, potassium, phosphorus
and zinc). This makes them
an excellent basic dietary
ingredient for adults and
children. Their sweet and
pleasant flavor is perfectly
suited to the preparation of
cookies, cakes, cereal bars,
creams and soups, both sweet
and savory. They have about
390 calories per every 100 g.

OAT

WINTER CHERRY

A member of the Nightshade family and a fruit of *Physalis alkekengi*, it is also known as the Chinese lantern for the delicate membrane that protects its bright orange, seed-rich mildly sour fruit. Rich in vitamin A, they help prevent eye disorders and have antioxidant properties thanks to their content of vitamin C. In addition, they seem to lower bad cholesterol levels. Winter cherries have 53 calories per 100 g.

The fruit of the *Persea gratissima* plant, avocado has a creamy pulp protected by shiny, dark green skin. It is rich in many unsaturated fats and omega 3, which aid the body in lowering bad cholesterol (LDL) levels in favor of good cholesterol (HDL). The presence of vitamins A, E and C, and of invaluable antioxidants such as lutein and zeaxanthin makes it an excellent health food. It has 230 calories per every 100 g. It is an excellent ingredient in sauces such as guacamole and salads. It can also be used to add creaminess to preparations in lieu of oil and butter.

AVOCADO

BROCCOLI

The broccoli, which belongs to the Cabbage family, is a flavorful and healthy inflorescence that matures in the fall. It is excellent steamed for a few minutes or, if very fresh, even raw in salads or juiced! In fact, it is best to eat it raw because this way all its beneficial compounds remain intact: folic acid to begin with, vitamin C, zinc, phosphorus, potassium, calcium, some sodium and, as if these are not enough, fiber, a lot of water and just 27 calories per every 100 g!

A fruit common in all tropical countries, the banana is easy to digest, moderately calorie rich (66 calories per every 100 g) and contains fiber that helps regulate bowel movements. Rich in minerals (potassium, phosphorus and calcium) and vitamins (C, B group, retinol and folic acid), it is a recommended snack for athletes and students. The simple and complex sugars it contains produce a pleasant feeling of fullness. It aids concentration and is also considered a natural anti-depressant thanks to its contents of tryptophan, which the body transforms into serotonin.

BANANA

CAULIFLOWER

One cannot talk about the large Cabbage family without mentioning the cauliflower in all of its varieties, which range in color from light green to bright purple. It has important beneficial properties, including cancer-fighting and anti-ageing properties. Specifically, cauliflower is recommended for athletes because it is rich in potassium and helps slow the oxidation of tissues thanks to its vitamin C contents. In addition, it is tasty and easy to prepare. Excellent raw on food platters, it is also great in juices. It is low in calories: 25 per every 100 g.

The beet *(Beta vulgaris)* is an annual plant of which the leaves and the bulb are consumed. It is easy to find in stores, steamed or baked. The root is easy to digest, nutritious, rich in potassium, folic acid, calcium, phosphorus, zinc and fiber, which help regulate bowel movements. It also contains saponins, which help burn fat. The few calories (20 per every 100 g) and large amount of water contained in beets, make them an excellent food for a fit lifestyle.

BEET

It is impossible to resist the charm of the fruit of *Prunus avium*, a member of the Rose family native to Europe, which seduces children and adults with its beautiful color, excellent flavor and outstanding properties. The fruit is characterized by a central pit and pulp of varying firmness (depending on the variety). Cherries are mildly laxative, diuretic, have few calories (38 per every 100 g) and contain potassium, which helps regulate blood pH and muscular function. They ripen from May to June and are ideal raw in juice or preserved as tasty jams or in syrup.

CHERRY

The fruit of the *Cocos nucifera* palm tree consists of an external, fibrous material covering an internal woody skin that encases the sweet and tasty white pulp. This fruit is very high in calories, lipids and fiber. It is a restorative fruit rich in potassium and capable of contributing to the reduction of bad cholesterol levels. Although rich in calories, it is a valid aid in weight loss diets because it dulls the appetite. Its pulp passed through a masticating juicer is a good substitute for milk and other beverages during a vegetarian or vegan diet due both to its pleasant flavor and its nutritional value.

COCONUT

Whatever chicory type you may prefer, it is sure to be low in calories (just 16 per every 100 g) and rich in water, potassium, calcium, phosphorus and vitamin C. In a diet, it is important for maintaining both a healthy weight and the proper function of the muscular and digestive systems. Chicory is cultivated but can also grow wildly on lawns in the spring. It has many different varieties of varying characteristics and shapes (escarole, Belgian endive, fall chicory, red and green grumolo to name a few) united by a distinct, somewhat bitter flavor. It is perfect in salads or juices, if you like sharp flavors.

CHICORY

CUCUMBER

The cucumber is one of the most consumed vegetables in the world (it is in fourth place behind tomatoes, onions and cabbage). It belongs to the Gourd family and is undeniably a summer vegetable because it is thirst-quenching, refreshing, diuretic, and rich in beneficial compounds such as potassium, phosphorus, calcium, zinc, silica, manganese and iron, and vitamins such as folic acid and vitamin C. It is low in calories, about 15 per every 100 g. Its beneficial properties are concentrated above all in its skin, which should be retained if not completely, then at least in part when used for cooking.

On the vegetable color wheel, carrots stand out for their magnificent, warm hues, which range from a yellow of variable intensity, to deep purple. This root is an important food to insert onto one's diet. In vegetable gardens, they ripen from May/June to October. However, they are available in grocery stores all year round. Incredibly rich in retinol, they are recommended for all who have vision or skin problems. They are excellent raw in salads or, even better, in juices that rehydrate, stimulate urine production and protect the stomach lining. They contain a lot of water and 33 calories per every 100 g.

CARROT

Fresh corn kernels are deliciously sweet. They have a texture that both children and adults love. They are rich in antioxidants and flavonoids. Compounds found in fresh corn help prevent cancer, relieve inflammation and slow ageing. While its contents of vitamin C and B group make it an excellent health food. Consumed as a vegetable above all in the Americas, corn ripens in the summer. However, it can easily be found for sale almost all year round.

CORN

The fruit of the *Opuntia ficus indica* is a berry full of seeds and rich, juicy pulp that varies in color from white to purple. Mexican in origins, it has been successfully introduced to the Mediterranean Basin. The fruit are rich in fiber and helpful in diets because they facilitate intestinal function and help keep intestinal flora healthy. They are energizing and thirst-quenching. Research has shown that they help maintain a healthy intestinal tract, combat parasites and facilitate the expulsion of kidney stones.

The fruit of the *Actinidia chinensis* plant is native to China and Japan but is now cultivated throughout the world with the largest crops being harvested in New Zealand and Italy. It ripens in the fall but can be found in stores throughout the year due to its long shelf-life. Kiwi is rich in potassium and vitamin C, compounds that are extremely useful to athletes and students. It stimulates digestion and promotes circulation. According to recent studies, it also combats tissue oxidation, prevents heart disease and relieves insomnia.

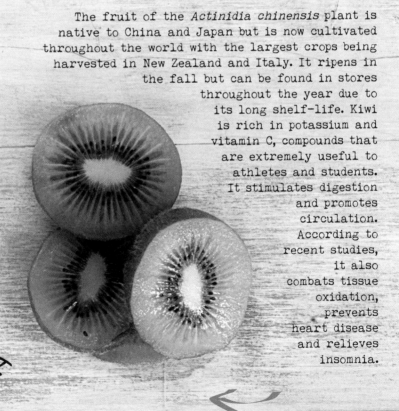

When they are ripe, figs have a delicate, soft skin, which encloses a sweet heart that melts in the mouth. These fruit are common throughout the Mediterranean Basin. Characterized by colors that go from green to pink, purple, blue and brownish, their pulp is rich and full of small seeds. Figs mature from June to September. In addition to being delicious to the taste, they contain enzymes that aid digestion, insoluble and soluble fiber, which promote bowel movements, and help fight bad cholesterol. They have 47 calories per every 100 g.

FIG

There are over a thousand varieties of strawberries, which can be found in grocery stores and vegetable gardens across the globe. Some produce fruit that are a joy to the nose and the palate several times a year, others, such as wild strawberries, only once. Small and particularly flavorful, the wild strawberry ripens in the spring. All strawberry varieties are rich in water, vitamin C, B group and the minerals calcium, potassium, iron and phosphorus.
Low in calories, they are diuretic and mildly laxative.

STRAWBERRY

A wheat variety that includes three species: *Triticum monococcum* (eincork wheat), *Triticum dicoccum* (emmer wheat) and *Triticum spelta* (spelt or dinkel wheat), all belonging to the Grasses family. The seeds have a membrane covering the kernel, which is not removed during refining. Farro contains a good amount of proteins, carbohydrates and fiber, useful for regulating bowel movements and burning fats. Easy to digest, it also helps lower bad cholesterol. Its gluten content makes it a poor choice for people suffering from celiac disease or protein intolerance.

FARRO

An aromatic fall/winter vegetable that is rich in water (about 93%), free of fat, low in sugars and proteins, It has a crunchy consistency and pure white color. The fennel has digestive properties, helps reduce bloating and prevent gas. Thanks to its contents of flavonoids and vitamin C, it has antioxidant properties and can help prevent joint pain. It is cleansing to the liver and lowers blood pressure. Some scientific studies have shown that fennel extract can inhibit the spreading of tumors and is useful during chemotherapy.

FENNEL

Recent scientific studies of this fruit have shown it to have antitumor properties due to its content of ellagic acid, which inhibits tumor cell growth. Raspberries are diuretic and depurative. They are recommended for heart burn. Their low-calorie content makes them ideal for diets (particularly if weight control is a goal) because they grant a pleasant sense of fullness despite having just 34 calories per every 100 grams. Their pleasant flavor improves fruit salads, smoothies and juices.

RASPBERRY

LEMON

The fruit of the *Citrus limon* tree is a treasure chest of beneficial properties. Its citric acid stimulates digestion; the limonene it contains can prevent cancer if consumed on a regular basis; and its flavonoids are excellent antioxidants. Thanks to its contents of vitamin C, it aids the production of collagen, which brightens skin, hydrates and facilitates the assimilation of iron. In addition to the juice, the rind of this fruit with its high contents of essential oils is perfect for flavoring many sweet and savory preparations.

BLACKBERRY

Whether wild (*Rubus ulmifolius*) or cultivated (*Rubus canadensis*), these berries grow on shrubs belonging to the Rose family. Studies have shown blackberries to be excellent anti-tumor agents thanks to their contents of anthocyanins. Sweet and juicy, they have diuretic and depurative properties. They are low in calories but rich in the vitamins C, E, A and K, as well as in potassium, calcium, phosphorus, zinc and iron. Blackberries have a lot of fiber, which is beneficial to digestion and intestinal flora.

The round, bright green fruit of the *Citrus aurantiifolia* tree, a member of the Citrus family, with its aromatic and thirst-quenching juice, is a wonderful health ally: its contents of vitamin C aid the immune system; its antioxidants combat free radicals and slow ageing; its citric acid promotes digestion and helps burn fats; and finally, it has antitumor properties (according to some studies). Its flavor is ideal for seasoning raw fish, sauces and cocktails.

LIME

A tropical fruit of the *Mangifera indica* tree, the mango is rich in beta carotene and has a delicious, sweet and aromatic flavor, which makes it suitable for both sweet and savory dishes. It has 57 calories per every 100 grams, contains fiber, vitamins C and E, folic acid, retinol and the minerals potassium, iron, phosphorus, calcium, zinc and sulfur. Research has shown it to have anti-tumor and antioxidant properties. However, mangos can also improve digestion, regulate bowel movements and soothe heartburn.

MANGO

An incredibly varied fruit, it exists in a range of sizes and colors that share the characteristic of prolonging our lives (an apple a day keeps the doctor away) and preventing tumor spread. Rich in water, fiber and sugars, it is a health aid that should always be within arm's reach. The perfect fruit for children's snacks and for decreasing the levels of bad cholesterol (LDL) with respect to those of good cholesterol (HDL). In addition, apples are beneficial to the heart thanks to their flavonoid contents and antioxidant properties. They also aid digestion and regulate bowel movements.

APPLE

POMEGRANATE

The fruit of the pomegranate tree is a berry filled with seeds composed of a woody pit surrounded by a sour, aromatic pulp that ripens in the fall, only on the plant. Fresh pomegranate juice is an excellent antioxidant, diuretic and digestion aid. Its astringent properties make it useful in cases of diarrhea. It can even improve the appearance of skin! The pomegranate should in introduced into the diet during the time of the year when it ripens (early fall), in order to prepare the body for the change in the seasons. It has 63 calories for every 100 g.

ALMOND

The nut of the almond tree is a magnificent seed that can be found for sale all year round. It is extremely energetic (containing 542 calories per every 100 g) and an important source of minerals (potassium, phosphorus, calcium, magnesium, iron, zinc and selenium) and vitamins E and A. Transformed into a beverage, this nut is extremely thirst-quenching as well as energizing. It can be a perfect substitute for milk, an animal-derived beverage, supplying many important nutrients. This makes it perfect for the lactose intolerant and for vegans.

LENTIL

A member of the Legume family, *Lens culinaris* is a small seed orange, green, brown or dark red in color. Generally, lentils are some of the most prized winter legumes because of the hardiness they bring to dishes! Rich in potassium, they are recommended for vegetarian and vegan diets and for athletes and students. Iron, phosphorus, calcium, magnesium and selenium are the minerals rounding out this legume's nutritional load, while its high content of fiber makes it a valid digestion aid.

BLUEBERRY

Blueberries are the fruit of *Vaccinium* L., a large shrub of which not just the berries, but also the leaves and the roots can be utilized. These berries are true treasures for our wellbeing: they aid digestion, prevent anemia, strengthen capillaries, and according to resent studies, contain anthocyanins which protect certain retinal pigments from degeneration. Low in calories, they are excellent whole or in beverages. Blueberries ripen in the summer and in addition to being great raw and whole, they make excellent jams and can be frozen and used to prepare sorbets.

HAZELNUT

The fruit of the common hazel were prized as far back as Ancient Greece and Rome, and have remained the foundation of many delicious preparations such as hazelnut spread, nougat and brittle to this day. They are extensively used in cuisine both toasted and raw in both sweet and savory preparations. The hazelnut is energizing, mineral-replenishing, high in protein, rich in lipids and fiber. It is an excellent source of calcium, potassium, phosphorus, zinc and vitamins such as group B, C, E, folic acid and retinol. There is only one tip to heed when eating them: don't exaggerate! They have 625 calories per every 100 grams.

MELON

The fruit of the *Cucumis melo*, member of the Gourd family, is extremely thirst-quenching, diuretic and gives a pleasant feeling of fulness. It is poor in calories (20 per every 100 g), but rich in the minerals potassium, calcium, phosphorus and vitamins A and C. It aids digestion and has refreshing properties. Rich in sugars, it is the perfect ingredient for fruit salads, sorbets and juices. In addition, it seems to thin the blood, which makes it a priceless ally in preventing heart attacks.

PEAR

The pear, a fruit of *Pyrus communis*, member of the Rose family, is available year-round. Its pulp is excellent for cold-pressed smoothies, producing a creamy, extremely aromatic beverage. Low in calories, 41 per every 100 g, it is easy to digest and contains fiber for regulating bowel movements. Recent studies have shown that its skin contains flavonoids, which are antioxidant, and cinnamic acid, which is believed to have anti-tumor properties.

CHILI PEPPER

Many recipes would be unthinkable without this priceless spice, which has a flavor that ranges from mild to incredibly spicy, transforming regular dishes into tasty specialties. Beverages can also benefit from this fresh spice, which can be used to transform fruit and vegetable juices into perfect appetizers and cereal containing beverages into flavorful preparations. Chili peppers are an important part of the diet. They are low in calories, rich in potassium, vitamin C and retinol. If they are not already part of your diet, it is best to introduce them to your meals gradually in order to better enjoy them and to choose your favorites among the many varieties.

Sweet peppers are rich in vitamin C, retinol and folic acid, which are invaluable for staying healthy. They are low in calories (22 per every 100 g), full of water and great for weight loss diets. They are members of the Nightshade family and can vary in color and shape: ranging from yellow to red and intense green. When purchasing, make sure they are plump and shiny, and that their stem is green. Just one fresh, raw pepper is sufficient to satisfy the required daily dose of vitamin C! Excellent antioxidants, they are versatile and easy to cook. They ripen at the end of the summer.

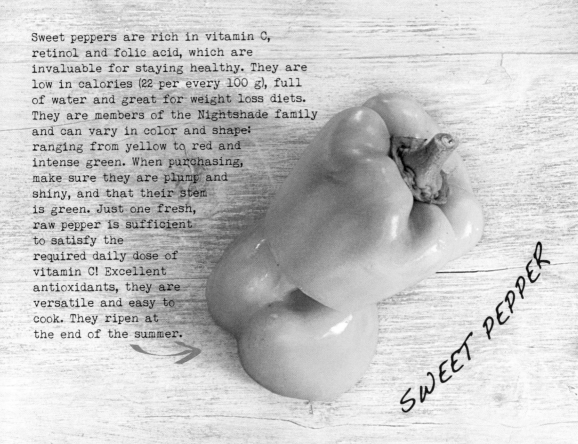

SWEET PEPPER

The papaya is a fruit with extremely sweet, soft and buttery pulp. In spite of this, it has few calories (just 36 per every 100 g), which makes it ideal for the preparation of delicate beverages. Only the pulp of the fruit is consumed; the skin and the seeds are discarded. In its native countries, such as Mexico and tropical countries, it is used in the preparation of stewed meat, sauces and salads. It contains an enzyme, papain, that can improve digestion. The presence of vitamins C and E, folic acid and retinol further add to the fruit's health value.

PAPAYA

Tomatoes, which belong to the Nightshade family, are a prized food during the hot months when they are consumed raw because they contain 94% water and with just 17 calories per every 100 grams, don't tire the digestive system. This makes them invaluable in weight loss diets. Rich in lycopene, they retain most of their antioxidant properties even when cooked. Following recent scientific studies, they have been recommended for the prevention of prostate cancer, cholesterol reduction and cell oxidation.

TOMATO

GRAPEFRUIT

The fruit of the *Citrus paradisi* plant, a member of the Citrus family, stands out for its aromatic rind and juicy, extremely thirst-quenching pulp. Diuretic and digestive, just one of these fruit is sufficient to satisfy the daily requirement of vitamin C. They contain many nutrients: from minerals including calcium, phosphorus, potassium, magnesium, zinc and selenium, to vitamins such as C, A, B group and E. In addition to their digestive and antiseptic properties, they protect the colon and promote good sleep.

PISTACHIO

A tasty nut with a characteristic shell protecting a soft, green seed, pistachios are decidedly calorific! They contain 562 calories per every 100 g. However, they also have a lot of beneficial properties: they hydrate dry skin, protect against eye disorders, help control cholesterol and promote the assimilation of iron due to their contents of copper. In addition, they contain calcium, phosphorus, zinc and potassium, a substance that is extremely important for athletes and the elderly.

The peach tree is also a member of the Rose family; its water-rich and calorie-poor (just 27 per every 100 g) fruit supplies an excellent amount of fiber and is mildly laxative. Yellow-fleshed peaches contain carotenoids and vitamin C. All varieties have anti-tumor properties, help neutralize free radicals and lower bad cholesterol levels (LDL) in favor of good cholesterol (HDL).

PEACH

In the preparation of beverages using a masticating juicer, this fruit can be used both fresh (plums) and dried (prunes), once re-hydrated. It is a treasure for intestinal health, especially for constipation sufferers because its mildly laxative properties stimulate bowel movements. Mineral-replenishing and reinvigorating, it is recommended for athletes, to replenish electrolytes lost to sweat, and for fatigue. Recent studies have shown them to help prevent osteoporosis in women that have gone through menopause. When preparing juices, you should be aware of the difference in calorie content: plums have 42 calories per every 100 g, while prunes have 220.

PLUM

RADICCHIO

Radicchio has a bitter flavor and a splendid purple color. It has a lot of fiber that can improve intestinal function, promote the production of bile and cleanse the liver. It is recommended for diabetics and for reducing free radicals. It is also useful in weight loss diets because it is filling. It contains a lot of water (about 94%) and not a lot of calories: 13 per every 100 g.

Brown rice is easy to digest, refreshing, detoxifying and gluten-free. This means it is recommended for celiac sufferers and the gluten-intolerant but also for weight loss diets because it grants a feeling of fullness while providing less calories than other foods. To prepare rice milk, the grains should be boiled and added to the masticating juicer with an equal amount of water; this beverage can also be used to dilute fruit and vegetable juices. Brown rice contributes to lowering bad cholesterol, combats free radicals and relieves insomnia.

BROWN RICE

An annual grass belonging to the Parsley family, celery helps lower high blood pressure and soothe inflammation of the stomach lining in cases of gastritis. The coumarin it contains impedes free radicals, while limonene and selinene promote urine production and vitamin C strengthens the immune system. It is an invaluable ally in the reduction of bad cholesterol (LDL) levels. The fiber it contains aids digestion and prevents constipation.

CELERY

Thought to have strong anti-oxidant properties, green tea is also believed to help repair oxidative cell damage. The daily ingestion of this beverage protects against heart attacks and strokes, and is the key to longevity! Recent studies have also shown that countries where green tea is a popular beverage have lower cancer rates. It is a recommended beverage for people who have trouble focusing and are experiencing fatigue because it improves concentration and provides a boost of energy.

GREEN TEA

SOY BEAN

Soy milk is often an excellent substitute for cow's milk, particularly for the lactose intolerant and for vegans. This little plant, belonging to the Legume family, is native to China, but is now cultivated in numerous other parts of the world. An excellent source of protein, the milk obtained from its soaked and boiled beans is an excellent base for beverages beneficial to our health. Soy beans have anti-tumor properties, relieve disorders linked to menopause and help lower bad cholesterol levels.

GRAPE

A juicy fruit that matures in the summer and fall, it is energetic and thirst-quenching. Grapes can be found for sale both fresh and dried (raisins). Fresh grapes have 61 calories per every 100 g, while raisins have 283. These berries are considered to have detoxifying and anti-inflammatory properties. The flavonoids they contain (quercitin and resveratol) combat free radical damage and slow aging. The nutritional characteristics of red and white grapes are similar. However, red grapes contain higher percentages of iron and flavonoids.

CELERIAC

The aromatic and tasty celeriac is a plant belonging to the Parsley family. It contains a lot of water (about 88%) and fiber, which speeds up digestion. According to recent studies, it aids bone mineralization and slows neuron damage. It is a valid aid during weight loss diets because drinking its juice before a meal dulls the appetite, reducing the number of calories consumed. In addition, it seems that the juice helps cleanse the liver. However, it is not recommended for people taking diuretics or blood thinners.

The immature fruit of *Cucurbita pepo* is an extremely useful vegetable in the diet because although it has very few calories (just 11 per every 100 g), the fiber it contains makes it very filling, which promotes weight loss. In addition, its consumption helps lower bad cholesterol levels. The zucchini is diuretic, easy to digest and relieves the symptoms of arthritis. Zucchinis ripen in the spring and summer but can be found all year round. However, it is best to use them in the warm months to get the maximum nutritional value.

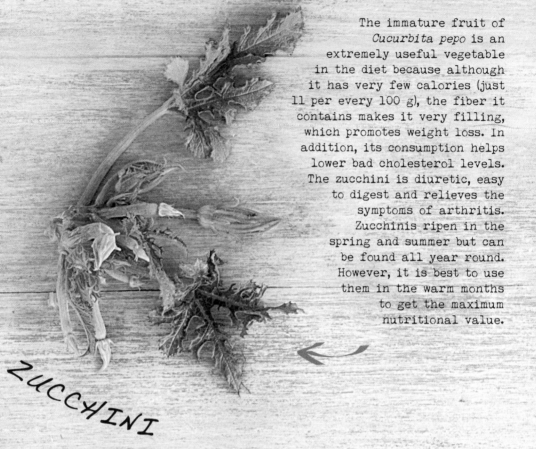

ZUCCHINI

PUMPKIN

A fall fruit belonging to the Gourd family, it is a must in any diet for the health benefits it brings. Mildly laxative, the pumpkin is also diuretic and refreshing. Despite its dense pulp, it is rich in water (about 95%), low in calories (about 18 per every 100 g) and contains calcium, potassium, phosphorus and large amounts of retinol. Pumpkin also seems to improve skin health and calm the nerves.

VANILLA

These aromatic pods, the fruit of the *Vanilla planifolia* plant, a member of the Orchid family, have often been thought to have aphrodisiac properties, although no scientific evidence of the fact has yet been found! However, their aroma and flavor have been proven to improve the quality of desserts and the mood, which makes them a recommended ingredient during depression. The compounds contained in these pods help slow oxidative damage by free radicals. The eugenol contained in their essential oil seems to aid in fighting infections.

Ginger stimulates digestion and has anti-inflammatory and antiseptic properties. The part of the plant typically used is the rhizome, fresh, grated, powdered or juiced. Its consumption aids the digestion of fats and animal proteins, and improves the flavor of foods. Its contents of gingerol help neutralize stomach acidity and prevent the formation of gas. Ginger is an excellent remedy for nausea; just chew a small piece of ginger to relieve the symptoms.

GINGER

Fruit-Based Preparations

Watermelon, cherries or blueberries to name a few; these, and all fruit in general, are the ingredients that have a special role to play in juices. Thanks to their high water contents, they can transform into a delightfully thirst-quenching, delicious beverages. If you use a masticating juicer, fruit juices will be richer in nutrients, vitamins and minerals. They will become truly capable of raising the quality of your diet and could be considered equal to whole fruit in their natural state. Naturally, it is always best to use ripe, aromatic and possibly organic fruit that is in season in order to get the maximum energy boost and all the benefits that the fruit can to offer. This section contains classic pairings, pairings for a pleasant, light breakfast, for a healthy snack or to help replenish fluids after intense physical activity.

Depending on the masticating juicer you have, fruit-based beverages can also be made using frozen ingredients, becoming valid substitutes for an after-meal sorbet or a dessert.

Peach Cream with Cocoa Powder and Hazelnuts

Servings

Difficulty

Prep Time
10 minutes

**Soaking
Time
1 night**

3/4 cup (100 g) raw, shelled hazelnuts - 2 ripe, organic peaches - 1 1/2 tbsp (10 g) unsweetened cocoa powder

1. Soak the hazelnuts in 2 cups (5 dl) of water for one night. Drain them and place into a masticating juicer. Activate, catch the beverage into a pitcher and place into the refrigerator until needed. You can increase the volume of the hazelnut milk based on the number of beverages you wish to prepare and dilute with water if desired.

2. Wash the peaches, cut without peeling and remove the pit. Juice in a masticating juicer and mix with the cocoa powder using a whisk. Add the hazelnut milk, mix once more and serve.

The consistencies and the water contents of the ingredients grant a pleasant sensation of freshness and creaminess. This cold-pressed juice is very thirst-quenching and nutritious. It can substitute a snack, leaving a pleasant feeling of lightness and fullness.

Coconut, Pineapple and Winter Cherry Cream

Servings

1 cup (400 g) coconut pulp – 1 organic apple – 1 2/3 cups (300 g) pineapple pulp – 12 winter cherries

Difficulty

1. Wash the fruit. Skin the pineapple, eliminate the core and chop into pieces small enough for the masticating juicer. Break the coconut pulp into pieces, the smaller the better. Cut the apple and remove the core.

2. Place 4 winter cherries aside for decoration and skin the others.

3. Mix the fruit together and transfer gradually into the masticating juicer. Catch the juice, mix and pour into glasses. Decorate every glass with the winter cherries and serve.

Prep Time
10 minutes

Depending on the filter you choose to use, you can make a cream that is more or less dense. Using a coarse-mesh filter you will obtain a mixture that can become a delicious, healthy and light sorbet if kept in the freezer for 20 minutes.

Apricot, Peach and Berry Cold-Pressed Juice

Servings

Difficulty

Prep Time
10 minutes

4 organic peaches - 4 frozen apricots - 1/4 cups (30 g) frozen blackberries - 1/4 cups (30 g) frozen blueberries

1. Let the frozen fruit thaw for 30 minutes at room temperature before using.

2. Wash and slice the peaches into wedges.

3. Remove the pits from the apricots and slice. Place into the masticating juicer with the peaches.

4. Catch the mixture into a pitcher. Rinse the filter and juice the berries (set 4 blueberries aside for decoration).

5. First pour the peach and apricot juice into the glasses then add the berry juice. Decorate with the blueberries and serve.

This beverage can be a refreshing, thirst-quenching and nutritious snack or even a dessert substitute.

Melon and Pineapple Cold-Pressed Juice

Servings

1 pineapple (weighing about 2 lb., 1 kg) – 1 melon (weighing about 2 lb., 1 kg) – 1 grapefruit

Difficulty

Prep Time
15 minutes

1. Wash the fruit. Cut the melon and remove the skin and seeds. Chop into pieces of suitable size for the masticating juicer.

2. Wash and peel the pineapple. Remove the core and chop.

3. Peel the grapefruit, remove the albedo (the white spongy material surrounding the segments) and split into segments.

4. Mix together and pass all the fruit through a masticating juicer equipped with a fine-mesh filter. Catch the juice in a pitcher.

5. Serve immediately to ensure none of the nutrients of the ingredients are lost.

Extremely thirst-quenching, this juice supplies an excellent amount of minerals and vitamins. It is particularly recommended after physical activity and helps reintegrate liquids lost on hot summer days.

Plum, Banana and Currant Cold-Pressed Juice

Servings

2 medium bananas - 2 1/4 cups (400 g) plums - 3/4 cup (100 g) currants

Difficulty

**Prep Time
10 minutes**

1. Wash the currants and the plums. Peel and slice the bananas. Place them into a container.

2. De-stem the currants (set two clusters aside for decoration) and add to the bananas.
Remove the pits from the plums and leave whole if they are small.

3. Place the fruit into a masticating juicer and catch the juice into a pitcher. Mix and serve.

4. Decorate the glasses with the currant clusters.

A magnificent, velvety preparation that is not too sweet thanks to the sour touch of the currants, it is thirst-quenching, nutritious and perfect for replenishing the minerals lost during physical activity and for dulling the appetite in a light and flavorful way.

Grapefruit and Orange Juice with Spices

Servings

Difficulty

Prep Time
10 minutes

1 yellow grapefruit – 2 oranges – 1 organic apple – 1/2 tsp (1 g) coriander seeds – 1/2 tsp (1 g) pink pepper – 1 fresh chili pepper of preferred spiciness

1. Wash the fruit and peel the grapefruit and oranges. Cut the apple into 4 parts and eliminate the seeds. Remove the stem and the (often very spicy) seeds from the chili pepper.

2. Place the chili pepper, citrus fruit, apple and half of the coriander seeds and pepper kernels into a masticating juicer. Catch the juice into a pitcher. You can dilute it with ice or cold water.

3. Pour the juice into glasses, sprinkle with the remaining spices and serve.

Extremely thirst-quenching and rich in vitamin C, this juice is recommended after physical activity or when you need to both rehydrate and have a light and tasty snack. The spices, which children and young adults usually do not enjoy, can be left out.

Watermelon, Pineapple, Apricot and Lemon Juice

7 oz. (200 g) pineapple − 14 oz. (400 g) watermelon − 6 apricots − 1 lemon

Servings

Difficulty

Prep Time
10 minutes

1. Peel the pineapple and chop into pieces. Check the user manual of your masticating juicer to make sure you can add the tougher sections of the fruit (the core of the fruit is fibrous and may damage the mesh of the filters), if not, eliminate it.

2. Take the watermelon pulp and chop without bothering to remove the seeds

3. Wash the apricots, divide into halves and remove the pits.

4. Peel the lemon and cut into 4 parts.

5. Place the fruit into the masticating juicer, pour the resulting juice into glasses and serve immediately.

In addition to supplying vitamin C, lemon also slows oxidation, preventing the beverage from changing color. This is a very thirst-quenching beverage. To render it more refreshing, add ice to taste.

Cherry and Plum Juice

Servings

2 cups (300 g) cherries – 1 cup (200 g) plums
– 1/2 peeled lemon

Difficulty

1. Wash the fruit. Pit the cherries and the plums.

2. Choose the filter you prefer for your masticating juicer: if you want a fluid, light beverage, use a fine-meshed filter, which catches most of the solids.

3. Juice all of the fruit in a masticating juicer. Catch the juice and pour into glasses.

4. Drink the juice right after juicing in order to enjoy all of the fruits' beneficial properties.

Prep Time
10 minutes

Use the discarded material and the juice of one orange or of a fruit in season of your choice to prepare a tasty liquid breakfast.

Strawberry, Blueberry and Orange Juice

Servings

2 oranges – 1 1/2 cups (200 g) strawberries – 1/3 cups (50 g) blueberries
For decoration: 2 wood skewers

Difficulty

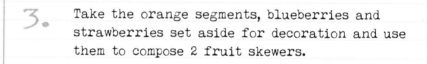

**Prep Time
10 minutes**

1. Wash the strawberries. Remove the stems and leave to drain until needed. Set two aside for decoration.

2. Peel the oranges, separate the segments and set 2 aside for decoration. Clean, wash and drain the blueberries. Set a few aside for decoration.

3. Take the orange segments, blueberries and strawberries set aside for decoration and use them to compose 2 fruit skewers.

4. Place all the fruit into a masticating juicer and catch the juice into a pitcher; mix and pour into glasses. Decorate with the fruit skewers and serve.

For a fluid, highly thirst-quenching juice, use a fine-mesh filter and if desired, add cold water or ice. If on the other hand you prefer a more velvety, denser texture, us a coarse-mesh filter, which will allow some of the pulp to pass through with the juice.

Apple, Pear, Banana and Lemon Juice

Servings

1 organic pear – 1 organic apple – 1 banana – 1 lemon – 1 grapefruit

Difficulty

Prep Time
10 minutes

1. Wash the pear and the apple. Peel the banana and slice into rounds. Place the rounds into a container and add the cored and chopped apple and pear.

2. Peel the citrus fruit, removing the albedo (the spongy, white sections that are lightly bitter and unpleasant to the taste), and break into segments. Combine all the fruit and place them into a masticating juicer.

3. Catch the juice with a pitcher and mix before pouring into glasses.

The differing textures and water contents of the fruit produce a beverage with a pleasant, refreshing creaminess. The juice is highly thirst-quenching and nutritious. It can substitute a snack, leaving you feeling refreshed and full.

Peach and Pear Juice

Servings

2 very ripe organic pears - 3 very ripe organic peaches
Optional: 1/2 lemon

Difficulty

1. Wash the peaches, cut into 4 or 8 parts depending on the size of the fruit and remove the pits.

2. Wash the pears, cut into 4 parts, remove the seeds and extract the juice in a masticating juicer immediately, because they oxidize very quickly.

3. Place the peaches into a masticating juicer as well. Catch the juice, mix and pour into glasses right away.

**Prep Time
5 minutes**

Extremely sweet, aromatic and velvety, this juice is a favorite with kids! If you wish to make it creamier, drizzle the chopped fruit with some lemon juice to prevent oxidation and freeze for 20 minutes before placing into the masticating juicer.
The resulting beverage will be reminiscent of a fruit sorbet and can substitute ice cream in a child's afternoon snack.

Grape and Melon Juice

Servings

2 3/4 cups (500 g) melon pulp - 3 1/2 cups (500 g) grapes
For decoration: 4 wood skewers

Difficulty

1. Wash the grapes and lay out to drain until needed. Set some aside for decoration.

2. Peel the melon, remove the seeds, skin, and any fibrous sections then chop.

3. Place into the masticating juicer a little at a time and catch the juice. Mix and serve accompanied by grape skewers.

**Prep Time
10 minutes**

Highly thirst-quenching, this juice has anti-inflammatory and diuretic properties. It is an ideal beverage for replenishing liquids lost to sweating and for filling up on minerals and vitamins. Melon is rich in retinol, a compound helpful in the summer when the sun tires out the skin. In fact, it stimulates the production of melanin.

Preparations with Vegetables and Fruit

Mixing fruit and vegetables is not only pleasant to the palate; these ingredients can substantially increase nutritional value and can include foods that are usually consumed cooked, which results in the loss of a good part of their vitamins and minerals. A raw, refreshing juice is a great resource. When the flavor of some of the ingredients is not very pleasant, fruit steps in, softening the bitterness of chicory, the spiciness of ginger, and the tanginess of beets. This section presents recipes rich in flavor and color; while pairing watermelon and cucumber is undeniably thirst-quenching, refreshing and light, combining coconut with corn and apple can substitute an entire meal for both adults and kids. When trying to lose weight, a creamy and smooth preparation of fruit and vegetables is a pleasant and satisfying resource for substituting a meal.

Sweet Pepper, Carrot, Orange and Apple Cream

Servings

Difficulty

Prep Time
15 minutes

1 large, red sweet pepper – 4 carrots – 2 oranges – 2 organic apples – 4 organic cucumbers – 10 oregano flower spikes
For decoration: 2 oregano flower spikes
Optional: 2 tbsp (20 g) extra virgin olive oil, salt, chili pepper powder

1. Wash the vegetables and the fruit. Remove the stem, seeds and white sections from the pepper. Chop it and place into a bowl. Add 1 peeled, chopped carrot, 2 oregano spikes and the oranges.

2. Place the cucumbers and one apple chopped into pieces small enough for the masticating juicer into another bowl.

3. Scrub the remaining carrots, chop and add to the remaining apple and 4 oregano spikes.

4. Place the pepper, oregano and oranges into the masticating juicer first. Catch the juice into a pitcher. Rinse the filter and add the cucumbers, apple and 2 oregano spikes. Catch the juice into a different container.

5. Last, add the carrots, apple and 2 oregano spikes without washing the filter.

6. Pour the juices from the different pitchers into each glass, starting with whichever juice you prefer and decorate with 2 oregano spikes.

Avocado, Lemon and Mango Cream

Servings

Difficulty

Prep Time
15 minutes

1 mango – 1 avocado – 1 lemon
For decoration: lemon leaves and mint sprigs

1. Peel the mango. Remove the pit, chop the pulp and place into a bowl. Peel the avocado, chop and add to the mango.

2. Peel the lemon leaving a thin layer of the albedo behind. Its mildly bitter flavor pairs perfectly with the sweet of the mango and the neutral of the avocado.

3. Place the ingredients into a masticating juicer with a coarse-mesh filter. Catch the puree into a pitcher. Mix and pour into glasses.

4. Decorate with lemon leaves and mint sprigs and serve right away.

Smooth and velvety, this cream has a delicious flavor and soft consistency. To ensure the beverage is rich in nutrients, all of the ingredients should be very ripe and free of brown spots, and the mango should be juicy and aromatic.

Beet, Corn and Lemon
Cold-Pressed Juice

Servings

1 cup (200 g) baked beets – 2 lemons – 3/4 cup (2 dl) corn milk – 2 green chili peppers – 3 thyme sprigs
For decoration: 2 lemon slices, 2 thyme sprigs and edible flowers
Optional: 1 tbsp (10 g) extra virgin olive oil, salt

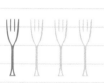

Difficulty

**Prep Time
10 minutes**

1. Wash the chili peppers and remove the stems, seeds and white sections (placenta) if you want to tone down the spiciness.

2. Peel the lemons and cut into pieces small enough for the masticating juicer. Wash the thyme and only keep the leaves.

3. Peel and chop the beets. Place into the masticating juicer together with the thyme, lemon and chili pepper. Catch the juice.

4. Mix with corn milk (see the "Seasoned Corn Milk with and Apples" recipe on pag. 132) and pour into glasses. Decorate with lemon slices, edible flowers and thyme sprigs.

An excellent beverage particularly suitable to students and athletes but also to people in need of a boost of energy and minerals or a hardy snack.

Blueberry, Raspberry, Carrot and Lemon Cold-Pressed Juice

Servings

3/4 cup (100 g) raspberries - 2/3 cup (100 g) blueberries - 1 carrot - 1 lemon - 1 grapefruit

Difficulty

1. Trim the berries. Wash them and lay out to drain until needed. If you would like a frozen beverage to serve at the end of a meal, leave the berries in the freezer for 30 minutes before use.

2. Peel the citrus fruit, removing the albedo; cut them into pieces small enough for the masticating juicer. Peel and chop the carrot.

3. Place the fruit and the carrot into the masticating juicer. Catch the juice into a pitcher. Mix and divide among the diners.

4. Serve it with water or ice. If you want to serve it as a dessert, let it sit in the freezer for 15-20 minutes before serving.

**Prep Time
10 minutes**

Blackberry, Apple, Carrot and Lemon Cold-Pressed Juice

Servings

2 organic apples - 3/4 cup (100 g) blackberries - 1 lemon - 2 carrots - water and ice to taste

Difficulty

**Prep Time
10 minutes**

1. Clean and wash the blackberries. Place them on a kitchen cloth to drain. Wash the apples. Cut them into fourths and remove the seeds.

2. Wash and peel the lemon. Remove most of the albedo (because it's bitter) and split into segments. Wash the carrots. Scrape them and chop.

3. Place the ingredients into the masticating juicer. If you prefer a creamy, somewhat dense beverage, insert a coarse-mesh filter. You can also dilute the beverage with water, ice or both.

Consume the beverage as soon as it is made to benefit fully from the ingredients. However, if you would like to conserve it, store in the refrigerator in an air-tight container and shake before drinking to re-mix the settled ingredients.

Coconut, Apple and Endive Juice

Servings

1 coconut – 2 apples – 1 small endive head

Difficulty

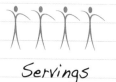

Prep Time
10 minutes

1. Wash the endive. Remove any damaged parts and set aside to drain until needed.

2. Cut the coconut pulp into small pieces. The smaller they are, the more juice the masticating juicer will be able to extract.

3. Wash the apples and remove the seeds and cores.

4. First, place the coconut into the masticating juicer. Catch the juice and set aside. If you are using a coarse-mesh filter, the liquid will be dense. You can dilute it with water if desired.

5. Next, place the endive and the apples into the juicer and catch the juice into a pitcher.

6. Pour the two liquids into glasses separately. Pouring first one juice and then the next will produce a beverage in which one color fades into the other.

Seasoned Cauliflower and Pomegranate Juice

Servings

10 oz. (300 g) white cauliflower - 1 pomegranate - 1/2 lemon
- 1 chili pepper - 1 tbsp (10 g) extra virgin olive oil
- salt and pepper
For decoration: 2 chili peppers

Difficulty

**Prep Time
15 minutes**

1. Trim the cauliflower. Wash it and cut into pieces small enough for the masticating juicer.

2. De-seed the pomegranate and gather the seeds into a bowl, making sure to remove all of the membrane that separates them because it is very bitter.

3. Set aside 2 thin slices of lemon that will be used for decoration and peel the rest of the fruit. Wash the chili pepper. Remove the seeds and the stem.

4. Place all the ingredients into a masticating juicer with a fine-mesh filter. Catch the juice into a pitcher.

5. Pour into glasses. Season with oil, salt and pepper. Decorate each glass with one lemon slice and one chili pepper.

An excellent, tasty and thirst-quenching beverage, it can be prepared using cauliflower of any color: green, orange or purple.
By using a coarse-mesh filter, you can obtain a delicious, dense condiment to serve with cereal dishes and raw or steamed vegetables.

Watermelon and Cucumber Juice

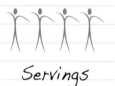

Servings

2 lb. (1 kg) watermelon - 2 cucumbers

Difficulty

1. Wash the cucumbers. Remove most of the skin and chop. Take the watermelon pulp and chop into pieces small enough for the masticating juicer without bothering to remove the seeds.

2. Place the ingredients into the appliance preferably with a fine-mesh filter to obtain a more fluid juice. Catch the liquid into an ice-cold pitcher to augment the refreshing power of this beverage.

Prep Time
5 minutes

If desired, add ice to taste and drink right away to enjoy all the beneficial properties that the ingredients can offer. Useful for rehydrating after a workout, this beverage helps prevent cramping that often plagues athletes and the elderly because of its potassium contents.

Chicory, Cucumber, Pineapple and Lemon Juice

Servings

10 oz. (300 g) pineapple – 3.5 oz. (100 g) chicory – 2 cucumbers – 1 lemon
Optional: 1 tbsp (10 g) extra virgin olive oil, salt and chili pepper

Difficulty

Prep Time
10 minutes

1. Wash and chop the chicory. Wash the cucumbers. Peel them half way and chop into rounds.

2. Remove the skin and the core from the pineapple. Chop it into small pieces.

3. Peel the lemon and slice.

4. Place the chicory leaves into the masticating juicer first, then the rest of the ingredients.

5. Catch the juice and if desired, season with 1 tablespoon (10 g) of extra virgin olive oil, a pinch of salt and a pinch of chili pepper.

Pineapple and lemon juice balance the mildly bitter flavor of the chicory, rendering the beverage pleasant to the taste. Chicory juice tends to be brownish in color. If you prefer it to be greener in color, use equal amounts of the ingredients.

Kiwi, Chicory and Lime Juice

Servings

4 kiwis – 3.5 oz. (100 g) chicory – 1 lime
Optional: salt, pepper and olive oil

Difficulty

1. Peel the kiwis and cut into slices.
   Soak the chicory then trim and drain.
   Peel the lime and cut it into slices as well.
   If you would like to decorate your glasses, set
   aside some chicory leaves and two kiwi slices.

2. Using a masticating juicer with a fine-mesh
   filter juice first the chicory then the lime
   and kiwi.

3. Catch the juice and season it if you intend to
   serve it as a cocktail, otherwise leave it as is.

Prep Time
10 minutes

Rich in vitamin C, retinol, folic acid, potassium and calcium,
this juice is definitely very useful for moments of fatigue
and for a boost of nutrients! The juice is dominated by
the sour and bitter flavors hence, it is not suitable to
children's palates.

Apple and Celery Juice

Servings

Difficulty

Prep Time
8 minutes

2 organic apples – 5 celery stalks – 1 lemon

1. Wash the apples. Remove the stems and the seed-containing cores. Cut into pieces small enough for the masticating juicer.

2. Trim the celery. Wash it, chop and add to the apples (set two stalks aside for decoration).

3. Peel the lemon. Cut into segments and add to the other ingredients.

4. Place the ingredients into a masticating juicer with a fine-mesh filter to obtain a fluid, light juice.

5. Catch the juice into a pitcher. Mix and pour into glasses. Decorate with the celery stalks, which can also be used to mix the beverage.

Celery is cleansing, diuretic, useful in cases of fluid retention and great in weight loss diets. It can also sooth rheumatic pain.

Pear, Orange and Ginger Juice

Servings

Difficulty

Prep Time
5 minutes

2 oranges – 2 organic pears – 1 ginger slice (about 0.1 oz. [2-3 g])
For decoration: 2 wood skewers and 2 ginger pieces

1. Cut 2 orange slices and set them aside for decoration. Peel and separate the segments. Wash the pears. Remove their seeds and cut into pieces small enough for the masticating juicer.

2. Place all the ingredients into the juicer and catch the juice into a pitcher; mix and pour into glasses. Prepare the decorations by threading a slice of orange and a piece of peeled ginger onto each skewer and serve.

Aromatic and thirst-quenching, this is a very pleasant beverage recommended for rehydrating, particularly during the winter. It is also great sipped during a workout.
The juice is an excellent snack, becoming a pleasant rehydrating break. If you can't find organic pears, peel them before juicing.

Pomegranate, Blackberry and Ginger Juice

Servings

2 pomegranates - 1 1/2 oz. (200 g) blackberries - 1/2 apple - 0.2 oz. (5 g) ginger - 1 lemon
For decoration: 2 wood skewers, 4 blackberries and 2 ginger pieces

Difficulty

Prep Time
20 minutes

1. De-seed the pomegranate. Remove the membranes from the seeds and place into a container.

2. Peel the lemon. Slice and add to the pomegranate seeds. Peel the apple and add to the other ingredients.

3. Clean the blackberries. Wash them, gently dry and add to the other fruit.

4. Peel the ginger and place it into the masticating juicer before the other fruit.

5. Catch the juice, mix and pour into glasses.

6. Prepare the decorative skewers by threading 2 blackberries and 1 piece of peeled ginger onto each.

Thirst-quenching, mineral-replenishing, nutritious, easily digestible and rich in vitamin C, this juice promotes urine production and can also be a tasty way of dulling the apatite! The only difficulty is de-seeding the pomegranate, which can be a labor-intensive and messy process because the seeds tend to break and squirt their juice. However, the goodness of the final result more than makes up for the trouble.

Vegetable-Based Preparations

This section contains preparations aimed at pleasing the palate, above all of adults who prefer savory, spicy and bitter flavors; these recipes can become more than just juices, but creamy soups that can be served as delicious, light and easily digestible first courses. Tomato with herbs can become a magnificent, healthy and aromatic cocktail; peppers are refreshing and thirst-quenching; while daikon and celery can transform into a hydrating, vitamin-rich beverage for a recharging break to the day. The ingredients that can be used to enrich your diet are numerous and various. The beverages they compose allow us to fill up on minerals and vitamins in ideal proportions, balanced to perfectly integrate the diet and support the body throughout the seasons. Naturally, cold-pressed juices should be consumed immediately to avoid oxidation, which not only alters the flavor but also affects nutritional value. It is also always best to use fresh vegetables that are in season and have not spent a lot of time in the refrigerator, and to cut them using ceramic knives to slow oxidation.

Seasoned Cucumber, Onion and Tomato Cream

Servings

2 cucumbers – 4 medium tomatoes or 12 cherry tomatoes – 1 purple onion – 7 chive stems – 7 purslane sprigs – 2 tbsp (20 g) extra virgin olive oil – 1/2 lemon – 2 fresh, moderately spicy chili peppers – salt
For decoration: 3 chive stems, 3 purslane sprigs, edible flowers

Difficulty

Prep Time
10 minutes

1. Wash the tomatoes. Wash the cucumbers as well and peel half of the skin so that the cream does not become too dark. Chop the vegetables into pieces small enough for the masticating juicer.

2. Peel the onion and chop. Wash the chili peppers.

3. Wash the chives and the purslane, removing any hard parts.

4. Place the tomatoes, cucumbers, onion and 2/3 of the chives and purslane into the masticating juicer. Catch the cream into a pitcher. Season with lemon juice, oil and salt to taste.

5. Mix the cream and pour it into single serving bowls. Season with freshly cut chili pepper rounds, decorate with aromatic herb sprigs and edible flowers, and serve right away.

Asparagus and Corn Cream

Servings

2 fresh corn cobs - 10 medium asparagus
Optional: salt and pepper

Difficulty

Prep Time
10 minutes

1. If you would like to prepare a light, refreshing and thirst-quenching cream, place the washed asparagus into the freezer for 15 minutes before extracting their juice.

2. Remove the kernels from the corn cobs and place into a bowl. Transfer into the masticating juicer with a fine-mesh filter together with the asparagus. Catch the juice into a pitcher.

3. If you would like to season the beverage, add salt and pepper. Mix and serve.

Use the remaining pulp to enrich soups, adding it along with other ingredients.

Fennel, Chicory and Zucchini Cream

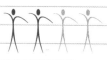

Servings

4 small, very fresh zucchinis - 1 fennel - 1.7 oz. (50 g) chicory

Optional: 2 tbsp (20 g) extra virgin olive oil, salt, chili pepper, 1 tbsp (15 g) lemon juice

Difficulty

**Prep Time
10 minutes**

1. Trim the chicory. Place it into a bowl with water and rinse several times to remove any traces of earth. Allow to drain.

2. Wash the fennel. Trim the green top and chop. If the outer layer is damaged or fibrous, discard it as well.

3. Wash the zucchinis. Trim the ends and cut into rounds.

4. Place the chicory into the masticating juicer. Follow with the fennel and the zucchinis. Catch the juice into a pitcher.

This aromatic, thirst-quenching and mildly bitter beverage is excellent as a tasty cocktail, especially if seasoned; its creaminess and velvety texture means that it can also be used as a dip for vegetable platters or as a sauce for boiled rice or steamed vegetables. It can also be a great thirst-quencher if diluted with water.

Purple Cabbage, Carrot and Avocado Cold-Pressed Juice

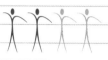

Servings

7 oz. (200 g) purple cabbage - 2 purple carrots - 2 tomatoes - 1 avocado - 1 lime - salt and pepper

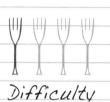

Difficulty

1. Wash all the vegetables. Peel the avocado and eliminate the pit. Scrape the carrots. Peel the lime and chop all the ingredients separately into pieces small enough for the masticating juicer.

2. Place the avocado into the juicer with the lime. Catch the juice into a container and set aside until needed. Follow immediately with the other ingredients. Catch the juice. Season the juices to taste before combining them.

**Prep Time
10 minutes**

3. To get multi colored beverages, pour the cabbage-based juice into the glasses first, then pour the avocado juice on top.

Use a toothpick to create images in the juice by gently dragging one juice towards the other, mixing them where needed. Serve the two-colored cream as a tasty and original cocktail or as an appetizer.

Zucchini, Radish, Carrot and Lime Cold-Pressed Juice

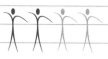

Servings

2 carrots - 2 zucchinis - 10 radishes - 1 lime - 1 slice of fresh ginger
Optional: 2 tbsp (20 g) oil - salt and pepper - icy water

Difficulty

Prep Time
10 minutes

1. Trim all the vegetables and wash all the ingredients.

2. Scrape the carrots and slice them. Trim the ends of the zucchinis and cut into rounds. Place a few slices of the vegetables aside for decoration. Peel the lime after having cut two slices for decoration.

3. Place all the ingredients into a masticating juicer. Catch the juice into a pitcher and divide among glasses.

4. If you would like to serve this beverage as a cocktail, season it to taste while it is still in the pitcher to ensure all the ingredients are mixed well.

5. Decorate the beverage with slices of lime and pieces of vegetables.

Seasoned Cabbage, Carrot and Celery Juice

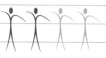

Servings

2 carrots - 7 oz. (200 g) curly cabbage - 1.7 oz. (50 g) celery - 2 tsp (6 g) extra virgin olive oil - 1 fresh chili pepper - 2 tbsp (30 g) lemon juice - salt

Difficulty

1. Wash the celery. Wash and peel the carrots. Break off the cabbage leaves, rinse them and drain. Wash the chili pepper and remove the stem.

2. Chop all the vegetables and place together into a masticating juicer with a fine-mesh filter, chosen to ensure the resulting juice is fluid and light.

Prep Time
10 minutes

3. Depending on how spicy you like your beverages, you can use some or all of the chili pepper.

4. Catch the juice into a pitcher. Season with oil, salt and lemon juice. Mix and serve.

Drink this beverage right away! It is a concentrate of vitamins (especially C and A). You can keep the leftover pulp from the juicer and use it to prepare or round out a soup. The fiber-rich pulp will be an excellent addition to a hot soup.

Seasoned Purple Cabbage, Radish and Daikon Juice

Servings

7 oz. (200 g) purple cabbage - 3.5 oz. (100 g) daikon
- 3.5 oz. (100 g) radish - 1 tbsp (15 g) lemon juice
- salt and pepper

Difficulty

1. Wash all the vegetables. Remove the leaves from the radishes. Scrape or peel the daikon. Chop the vegetables into pieces small enough for the masticating juicer.

2. Place the vegetables into the appliance and catch the juice into a pitcher. Season it with lemon juice, salt and pepper to taste.

Prep Time
10 minutes

This beverage is full of vitamins and minerals: the minerals calcium, phosphorus, potassium and sodium; and vitamins such as C and A. Daikon is thought to aid the burning of fats and urine production, hence it is recommended for weight loss diets.

Seasoned Daikon and Radish Juice

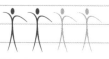

Servings

7 oz. (200 g) daikon – 10 radishes – 1/2 lemon – 4 mint leaves – 1 small tarragon sprig – salt and pepper – 1 tbsp (10 g) extra virgin olive oil
For decoration: edible leaves and flowers to taste

Difficulty

Prep Time
10 minutes

1. Wash the daikon and the radishes. Scrape them to eliminate any traces of earth.

2. Cut into pieces small enough for the masticating juicer.

3. Peel the lemon and cut it into pieces small enough for your appliance as well.

4. Place the mint leaves, tarragon, bulb vegetables and lemon into the juicer.

5. Catch the juice. Season it with pepper, salt to taste and oil. Mix and serve.

Mouthwatering and light, this juice is an excellent summer beverage, when one needs liquids to rehydrate and when the appetite needs to be stimulated. Refreshing and thirst-quenching, it is particularly suited to an adult's palate. This beverage can also be used to dilute tomato, cabbage or sweet pepper based preparations.

Broccoli Juice with Sweet Bell and Chili Peppers

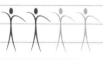

Servings

10 oz. (300 g) broccoli - 7 oz. (200 g) cauliflower - 2 small, green bull's horn peppers - 1 fresh chili pepper - 2 tsp (6 g) extra virgin olive oil - 2 tsp (10 g) lemon juice - unrefined Alaea salt
For decoration: 2 small wood skewers, 4 pitted olives and 1 chili pepper

Difficulty

Prep Time
10 minutes

1. Trim the broccoli and the cauliflower. Break off the florets from the central stems with your hands. Soak for 2 minutes then rinse. Wash the peppers. Remove the stems, seeds and white sections. Break into pieces small enough for the masticating juicer.

2. Wash the chili peppers.

3. Place all the ingredients into a masticating juicer with a fine-mesh filter. Dose the chili pepper based on how spicy you want the beverage to be.

4. Catch the juice into a pitcher and season with oil, lemon juice and salt. Prepare the skewers using pieces of chili pepper and olives; in addition to decoration, they will serve as stirrers for the juice, transferring some of their aroma to the liquid. Pour, decorate and serve right away.

You can also offer this beverage as an excellent, tasty cocktail that is rich in vitamin C.
Keep the pulp left in the juicer and use it to add flavor to vegetable stews.

Carrot and Radicchio Juice

Servings

4 purple carrots – 1 Belgian endive – 1 radicchio – 10 chive stems – 1 tbsp (10 g) oil – salt and pepper

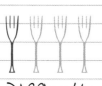

Difficulty

Prep Time
5 minutes

1. Soak the leafy vegetables then detach the leaves one at a time and set aside to drain in a colander until needed.

2. Wash the carrots. Scrape them or peel then cut into rounds.

3. Place the leafy vegetables (setting a few leaves aside for decoration) along with 8 chive stems into the masticating juicer first. Follow with the carrots. Catch the juice, mix it with oil, salt and pepper and pour into glasses.

4. Decorate each glass with the leaves set aside and 1 chive stem. Serve right away.

This pleasant, mildly bitter beverage is extremely thirst-quenching. It is best not to leave any of this juice for later, to ensure none of the nutrients are lost or the flavor is altered.

Sweet Pepper, Cucumber and Celery Juice

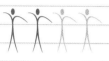

Servings

2 red sweet peppers - 2 cucumbers - 4 celery stalks
Optional: ice - salt and pepper

Difficulty

Prep Time
10 minutes

1. Wash the vegetables. Remove the stems, white sections and seeds from the peppers. Cut them into pieces small enough for the masticating juicer.

2. Wash the cucumbers and remove some of the skin. It is often indigestible despite being rich in nutrients; hence, experiment a little to determine the right amount for your stomach! Cut them into pieces.

3. Wash the celery. Place all the ingredients into a masticating juicer, using a fine-mesh filter to obtain a fluid and light, highly thirst-quenching juice that can be sipped like water.

4. If you would like to season it, add salt and pepper. If, on the other hand, you prefer it cool, add some ice.

An excellent summer drink, in addition to quenching your thirst, it supplies vitamins and minerals without requiring prolonged periods of digestion. It is a great way to rehydrate during hot summer days or after a workout.

Tomato, Basil and Oregano Juice

Servings

14 oz. (400 g) very ripe, organic tomatoes - 20 small basil leaves - 4 fresh oregano tops - 2 tbsp (g) extra virgin olive oil - salt and pepper
For decoration: aromatic herbs to taste

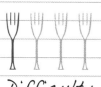

Difficulty

1. Soak the basil and the oregano in cold water then set aside to drain until needed.

2. Wash the tomatoes well. Remove the stems and any hard, fibrous sections. Chop into a bowl and place into the masticating juicer after the aromatic herbs.

3. Season the juice with salt, pepper and oil. Mix and serve.

Prep Time
5 minutes

Extremely pleasant as a cocktail or a refreshing and light first course, it is the perfect summer beverage.
This preparation is also delicious transformed into small popsicles (prepared in ice trays, for example) and used to add flavor to vegetable juices and legume or cereal dishes, adding a touch of color and aroma.

Celeriac, Carrot and Endive Juice

Servings

7 oz. (200 g) celeriac - 0.35 oz. (10 g) red carrots - 1 red Belgian endive - 3.5 oz. (100 g) endive - 2 red chili peppers of preferred spiciness
Optional: 2 tbsp (20 g) extra virgin olive oil, salt, 1 tbsp (15 g) lemon juice

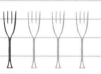

Difficulty

1. Wash the celeriac. Remove the hard sections (skin and roots) then slice. Peel the carrots and slice.

2. Wash the chili peppers and chop them, removing the stems and seeds if you want to tone down the spiciness.

3. Wash the greens and detach the leaves from the cores.

Prep Time
8 minutes

4. To get a fluid, light and highly thirst-quenching juice, place all the ingredients into a masticating juicer with a fine-mesh filter. Catch the liquid into a pitcher.

5. If you wish, season with salt, oil and lemon juice.

Preparations with Cereals, Nuts and Legumes

While fruit and vegetables are classic ingredients in home-made juices, almonds, hazelnuts, pumpkin seeds, soy, rice, farro, oat and barley are important new ingredients that can transform a regular beverage into a health drink. In a masticating juicer, nuts, cereals and legumes are transformed into beverages of various densities that are just as valid as those found on the shelves of health stores. On their own or with other ingredients, they are a magnificent dietary resource. Prepping these ingredients requires a little more time and experimentation, in order to ensure the final product is pleasant to the palate and highest in quality. Green tea with rice cream can become a delicious dessert that is excellent for your health; spiced millet cream can be a perfect appetizer or a delicious cocktail; and cold-pressed lentils can become an original first course. Our recipes are meant to provide inspiration for enriching your meals with creativity, warmth and flavor.

Vanilla Flavored Oat Cream

Servings

1 cup (200 g) oat groats – 20 shelled almonds – 2 vanilla pods – 1 1/4 tbsp (10 g) sunflower seeds

Difficulty

Prep Time
10 minutes

Cooking Time
30 minutes

Soaking Time
10 hours

1. Soak the oats and the almonds in 4 1/4 cups (1 l) of water for 10 hours.

2. Boil them in 4 1/4 cups (1 l) of water for 30 minutes together with the vanilla pods in pieces and the sunflower seeds.

3. Once cooked, drain and set aside a small amount of the cooking liquid; place the oat mixture into a masticating juicer, adding 2 cups (1/2 l) of the cooking liquid to aid in the extraction.

4. Catch the cream and divide among the diners.

The oat cream is hardy and nutritious, perfect as a breakfast or as a healthy substitute for dessert. Captivating and mouthwatering in flavor, it is rich in lipids, which help prevent oxidative damage. If you would like to sweeten it (although oats are naturally sweet, as are almonds), you can add wildflower honey or malt.

Turmeric Flavored Millet and Apple Cold-Pressed Juice

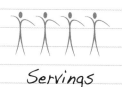

Servings

1/2 cup (100 g) millet - 4 organic apples - 2 tsp (6 g) turmeric

Difficulty

Prep Time
10 minutes

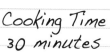

Cooking Time
30 minutes

1. Boil the millet in 4 1/4 cups (1 l) of water for 30 minutes; one minute before turning off the heat, add the turmeric and mix. Allow to cool in the cooking liquid.

2. Wash the apples and chop them shortly before using to prevent browning.

3. Once the millet has cooled, transfer it and its cooking liquid into the masticating juicer. Catch the resulting cream.

4. Cut the apples, place into the appliance and pour the juice into a container.

5. Add some or all of the millet milk (as preferred) to the apple juice. Mix and serve.

Appetizing and tasty, this beverage can replace an appetizer or a light first course. Millet has many virtues including high contents of proteins, sugars and fiber, which helps regulate bowel movements.

Oat and Fig Cream with Raisins

Servings

3 1/2 cups (200 g) of oats – 2 tbsp (20 g) sultanina raisins – 8 ripe figs

Difficulty

1. Soak the raisins and the oats in 2 cups (1/2 l) of water for 10 hours or overnight then boil for 30 minutes and allow to cool.

2. Wash the figs and cut into halves.

3. Place the oats into the masticating juicer first, without draining. Catch the cream into a container and set aside. Follow with the figs and catch the liquid into a different container.

**Prep Time
10 minutes**

4. Split the mixture among 4 glasses, filling them half way. Use the fig cream to fill the rest of the way.

**Cooking Time
30 minutes**

**Soaking
Time
10 hours**

*If you would like to use this beverage to replace a dessert, place it in the freezer for 20 minutes before serving.
Oat and fig cream is a hardy, energizing and healthy breakfast, recommended for students and all who carry out work that requires a lot of concentration.*

Farro Cream with Prickly Pear and Beet Juice

Servings

Difficulty

Prep Time
15 minutes

Cooking Time
30 minutes

Soaking Time
1 night

1/2 cup (100 g) farro – 2 prickly pears – 1 beet – 1 lemon – 1/2 grapefruit – 1/3 orange

For decoration: 2 winter cherries

1. Soak the farro for one night then boil in 4 1/4 cups (1 l) of water for 30 minutes. Allow to cool before draining.

2. Once the farro is cool, transfer it into the masticating juicer. The cream can be stored in a sealable bottle in the refrigerator for a few days. Hence, you can prepare it in advance.

3. Peel the beet, the prickly pears, the lemon, the orange and the grapefruit and place into the masticating juicer. Catch the juice into a pitcher.

4. Mix the juice before adding to the farro cream; if you wish, dilute with water for a more thirst-quenching beverage.

5. Decorate the glasses with winter cherries and drink for breakfast to get a rehydrating and nutrient-rich blast of energy.

Pistachio, Coconut and Banana Cream

Servings

3.5 oz. (100 g) coconut – 1 banana – 30 raw pistachios

Difficulty

**Prep Time
15 minutes**

**Soaking
Time
60 minutes**

1. Chop the coconut into small pieces and place them into a masticating juicer with a fine-mesh filter. Catch the juice into a container.

2. Shell the pistachios, place them into a bowl. Fill with the coconut juice and let the nuts soften for one hour.

3. Peel the banana and place into the masticating juicer. Add pistachios and coconut juice mixture a little at a time.

4. Catch the liquid in a pitcher and mix until the color and flavor are homogeneous before serving.

Nutritious, revitalizing and delicious, this beverage is a magnificent mid-day snack for adults and children. It is also a great way to recover energy lost during a workout.

Seasoned Corn Milk with Apples

Servings

2 fresh corn cobs - 2 organic apples - 1 tbsp (10 g) extra virgin olive oil - salt and pepper

Difficulty

1. Remove the kernels from the corn cobs and place into a bowl. Soak for a minimum of 3 hours in 2 cups (1/2 l) of water. Next, place the kernels into a masticating juicer along with the soaking water.

2. Catch the liquid into a sealable container and dilute with more water if it is too dense for your taste.

Prep Time
20 minutes

3. Wash the apples, cut into pieces small enough for the masticating juicer and place into the appliance.

4. Catch the juice and mix with the corn milk. Season with oil, salt and pepper to taste.

Cooking Time
120 minutes

Soaking
Time
3 hours

You can also prepare corn milk using dried corn. In this case, in addition to soaking the kernels you will need to boil them in water for at least 2 hours. Corn milk can be stored in the refrigerator for a few days.

Almond, Rice and Walnut Cream

Servings

3/4 cup (100 g) shelled almonds – 1/2 cup (100 g) white rice – 1/2 cup (50 g) shelled walnuts

Difficulty

Prep Time
20 minutes

Cooking Time
20 minutes

Soaking Time
8 hours

1. Wash the rice and boil in 2 cups (1/2 l) of water for 20 minutes then turn off the heat and allow to cool.

2. Place the rice and its cooking liquid into a masticating juicer and catch the cream. If the appliance has trouble extracting the liquid due to its density, gradually add 1 glass of water.

3. Soak the almonds and the walnuts for 8 hours then drain. Place into a masticating juicer and catch the cream. If the resulting liquid is too dense and compact, dilute it with some of the rice milk prepared beforehand.

4. Right before serving, mix the two liquids together and pour into glasses.

You can store the cream for as much as two days in the refrigerator in an air-tight container. This beverage can be diluted with cold water if desired.

Rice, Cauliflower and Chili Pepper Cream

Servings

Difficulty

Prep Time
10 minutes

Cooking Time
30 minutes

1/2 cup (100 g) brown rice – 10 pitted olives – 7 oz. (200 g) cauliflower – 4 chili peppers of preferred spiciness – salt
For decoration: 2 wood skewers, 4 pitted olives, 2 chili peppers

1. Boil the rice for 30 minutes in 2 cups (1/2 l) of water and allow to cool. Transfer into the masticating juicer without draining. Catch the cream into a container.

2. Trim the cauliflower. Wash it and cut into pieces. Remove the stems and seeds from the 2 chili peppers.

3. Prepare 2 skewers using 2 olives and 1 chili pepper for each.

4. Without changing the filter, extract the juice form 10 olives, the chili peppers and the cauliflower. Catch the liquid and mix with all or some of the rice cream. Salt to taste, pour into glasses, decorate with the skewers and serve.

This beverage is an excellent, light, tasty and very flavorful substitute for a first course.
It also makes a great sauce for steamed or raw vegetables.

Azuki Bean Milk with Beet and Chicory Cold-Pressed Juice

Servings

1/2 cup (100 g) azuki beans - 3.5 oz. (100 g) chicory - 1 cup (200 g) baked beets - 1 lemon

Difficulty

Prep Time
10 minutes

1. Prepare the azuki bean milk: Soak the legumes overnight and boil in 4 1/4 cups (1 l) of water over low heat for 3 hours. Allow to cool.

2. Once the beans are cool, place them and their cooking liquid into a masticating juicer with a fine-mesh filter.

3. Wash the chicory. Peel and chop the lemon and the beets.

4. Place them into the masticating juicer. Catch the resulting liquid and mix with the azuki milk.

Cooking Time
180 minutes

Soaking Time
1 night

You can also prepare larger amounts of the bean milk to use in the preparation of more beverages. Azuki beans have a delicious flavor that tends towards the sweet. They are perfect for both sweet and savory dishes. If desired, you can season the beverage with oil and pepper. Before using azuki bean milk, you must mix it well because the solids it contains tend to sink to the bottom.

Lentil Milk with Carrot and Chili Pepper Cream

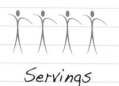

Servings

1 cup (200 g) lentils - 2 carrots - 2 hot chili peppers - 2 tbsp (20 g) extra virgin olive oil - salt, pepper

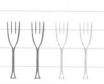

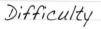

Difficulty

Prep Time
15 minutes

Cooking Time
120 minutes

1. Wash the lentils and cook for 2 hours in 4 1/4 cups (1 l) of salted water. Turn off the heat and allow to cool uncovered.

2. Wash the carrots. Peel them and chop. Wash the chili peppers and remove their stems. Drain the lentils, place into the masticating juicer and catch the resulting cream into a pitcher.

3. Extract the juice from the carrots and the chili peppers into a different container.

4. Before serving, pour the lentil milk into cups. Pour the carrot and chili pepper juice on top.

5. Season with salt, pepper and oil, and serve.

If you want a creamier beverage to serve as a first course, use a coarse-mesh filter.

Almond and Hazelnut Milk
with Mango and Papaya Juice

Servings

1 1/2 cups (200 g) shelled hazelnuts – 3/4 cup (100 g) shelled almonds – 1 medium mango – 1 small papaya (about 1.25-1.5 lb. [600-700 g]) – 8 cardamom pods

Difficulty

Prep Time
20 minutes

Soaking
Time
8-10 hours

1. Soak the hazelnuts and the almonds for 8-10 hours in 2 cups (1/2 l) of water.

2. Drain and place into a masticating juicer with a coarse-mesh filter. Because nuts are poor in liquids, they tend to clump together in the appliance. Hence, aid the process by adding 1 cup (1/4 l) of water. Catch the cream into a sealable bottle.

3. Peel the mango and remove the pit. Peel the papaya and remove the seeds. Chop all the fruit. Place the fresh fruit into a masticating juicer and catch the juice into a pitcher.

4. Add the hazelnut and almond milk to the juice to taste. Mix and add 2 cardamom pods per person, crushing them first so they release their aroma.

Hazelnut and almond milk can be stored in the refrigerator in an air-tight bottle for 2-3 days without spoiling.

Pear, Date, Sunflower Seed Cold-Pressed Juice with Almond Milk

Servings

2 pears – 10 dates – 2 1/2 tbsp (20 g) sunflower seeds – 1/2 cup (100 g) almond milk (see " Almond and Hazelnut Milk with Mango and Papaya Juice" on pag. 142)

Difficulty

1. Soak the sunflower seeds in hot water for 30 minutes then drain. Pit the dates.

2. Wash the pears. Remove their seeds and cut into pieces small enough for the masticating juicer.

3. Place the sunflower seeds into the masticating juicer first, follow with the dates and finish with the pears. Catch the juice, which will be very creamy, soft and similar to a puree. You can cool it in the refrigerator and serve it as a dessert.

4. Add almond milk to the date and pear cream until the desired thickness is achieved. Mix and enjoy!

Prep Time
10 minutes

Soaking Time
30 minutes

Ideal for a rich, nutritious and healthy breakfast, this beverage is an excellent meal for students, athletes and for people looking for an energetic but light beverage.

Soy Milk with Cold-Pressed Raspberry Juice

Servings

1 cup (200 g) yellow soy beans – 1 1/2 cup (200 g) raspberries – 1 vanilla pod – 1 tbsp (15 g) honey

Difficulty

Prep Time
10 minutes

Cooking Time
120 minutes

Soaking Time
10 hours

1. Soak the soy beans overnight or for about 10 hours then boil in 4 1/4 cups (1 l) of water along with the vanilla pod in pieces for about 2 hours over low heat. Soy milk can be stored in the refrigerator for a few days, hence you can prepare it in advance.

2. Once the soy beans are cooked, turn off the heat and allow to cool in the cooking liquid. Drain but set aside some of the cooking liquid. Place into a masticating juicer with a coarse-mesh filter adding small amounts of the cooking liquid when needed. Catch the liquid and store in a sealable container until needed.

3. Clean the raspberries and extract their juice in a masticating juicer with a coarse-mesh filter. Catch the juice into a pitcher, add the honey and mix with the soy milk in proportions of your choosing.

Vanilla is the ingredient of choice for improving the aroma and flavor of soy milk.
You can also use dates for a sweeter beverage, or salt and pepper for a more savory version.
In addition to serving it as a snack or breakfast, you can serve this beverage as a dessert.

Soy and Pine Nut Milk with Chili Peppers

Servings

Difficulty

Prep Time
10 minutes

Cooking Time
2-3 minutes

Soaking
Time
30 minutes

1 1/4 cups (300 g) soy extract, plain or seasoned with salt (see "Soy Milk with Cold-Pressed Raspberry Juice" on pag. 146) - 1/4 cup (30 g) pine nuts - 2 chili peppers - 1 tsp (3 g) curry powder

1. Dissolve the curry in 1/4 cup (50 g) of soy milk. Cook the mixture for 2 to 3 minutes to blend the flavors then allow to cool.

2. Soak the pine nuts in 1/2 cup (100 g) of soy milk (set aside 5-6 for decoration). After 30 minutes, place into the masticating filter with a coarse-mesh filter without draining. Next, mix the curry mixture with the pine nut cream.

3. Transfer into glasses and top off with the remaining soy milk. Decorate with chili peppers and serve.

Preparing beverage bases using legumes, nuts or cereals in advance allows to experiment with beverages of different consistencies and densities; beverages that can be diluted to taste and flavored with spices, herbs or anything your fantasy and personal taste can devise.

Coconut and Pumpkin Cold-Pressed Juice with Pumpkin Seeds and Chili Pepper

Servings

7 oz. (200 g) pumpkin - 1/4 cup (30 g) pumpkin seeds - 3.5 oz. (100 g) coconut - 2 fresh chili peppers of preferred spiciness

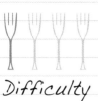

Difficulty

1. Soak the pumpkin seeds in 1/2 cup (1 dl) of warm water for 30 minutes then drain.

2. Remove the skin and any fibrous parts from the pumpkin.

3. Chop the coconut, place it into the masticating juicer and catch the resulting liquid into a container.

4. Remove the stem and seeds from the chili peppers.

Prep Time
10 minutes

5. Extract the juice from all the ingredients in a masticating juicer in the following order: pumpkin seeds, chili peppers, pumpkin pulp.

Soaking Time
30 minutes

6. Catch the juice into a pitcher and add to the coconut juice. Mix and serve.

An excellent, tasty and nutritious beverage for boosting your energy supply, it is a perfect appetizer, first course or fancy cocktail. The combination of sweet and spicy flavors makes this beverage particularly stimulating when appetite is low.

Pomegranate, Grape and Hazelnut Juice

Servings

1 pomegranate – 1 bunch of grapes weighing about 10 oz. (300 g) – 1/4 cup (30 g) presoaked hazelnuts

Difficulty

1. De-seed the pomegranate and place the seeds into a bowl. Wash the grapes and remove from the stems. Add to the pomegranate seeds.

2. Extract the juice first from the hazelnuts and then the other fruit. Mix and serve.

Prep Time
20 minutes

You can add water or ice to taste before serving in order to increase the thirst-quenching qualities of this beverage. This drink is diuretic, detoxifying, nutritious and rich in vitamins such as E, A and group B.
Its high potassium contents make it ideal for athletes, the elderly and people leading very active lives.

Green Tea with Rice Cream

Servings

Difficulty

Prep Time
10 minutes

Cooking Time
30 minutes

1/2 cup (100 g) white rice - 2 tsp (6 g) green tea powder - 2 tsp (10 g) honey - 1 vanilla pod

1. Bring the rice with the vanilla bean in pieces to a boil in 4 1/4 cups (1 l) of water. The vanilla will add aroma to the beverage and a pleasant flavor.

2. Simmer for 30 minutes then turn off the heat and allow to cool.

3. Once it is cool, place into the masticating juicer and catch the liquid into a sealable bottle.

4. Right before serving, add about 200 g of the rice milk to the green tea and honey. Mix and enjoy.

Rice milk, the density of which can be altered by changing the juicer's filter, can be stored for a few days in the refrigerator and diluted with water in amounts that can be varied depending on whether a lighter or a hardier beverage is preferred.
An excellent mid-day snack or a fancy dessert, this beverage is not only tasty but also healthy, stimulating and energizing without having too many calories.

The Author

CINZIA TRENCHI is a naturopath, freelance journalist and photographer, who specializes in nutrition and food and wine itineraries. She has collaborated in the drafting of many cook books published by both Italian and foreign publishing houses. A passionate cook, she has also worked for many years with various Italian magazines, writing articles about regional, traditional, macrobiotic and natural cuisines, supplying photographs and proposing dishes of her own creation. Her cook books suggest original, creative diets with unique dishes featuring flavor combinations and unusual pairings that take into account the nutritional properties of the ingredients, bringing balance and the subsequent improvement in wellbeing to every meal. She lives in Monferrato, in the Piedmont Region, in a house immersed in greenery. The flowers, aromatic herbs, fruits and vegetables from her garden serve as decorations for dishes and ingredients in original sauces and condiments, which she creates allowing herself to be guided by the changing seasons and a deep understanding of all the earth has to offer. In recent years, with much passion and creativity, she has put together several books for White Star Publishers.

Index of Ingredients

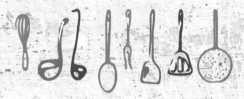

WHITE STAR PUBLISHERS

WS White Star Publishers® is a registered trademark
Property of White Star s.r.l.

© 2018 White Star s.r.l.
Piazzale Luigi Cadorna, 6
20123 Milano, Italy
www.whitestar.it

Translation and Editing: TperTradurre s.r.l.

ISBN 978-88-544-1241-5
1 2 3 4 5 6   22 21 20 19 18

Printed in Poland

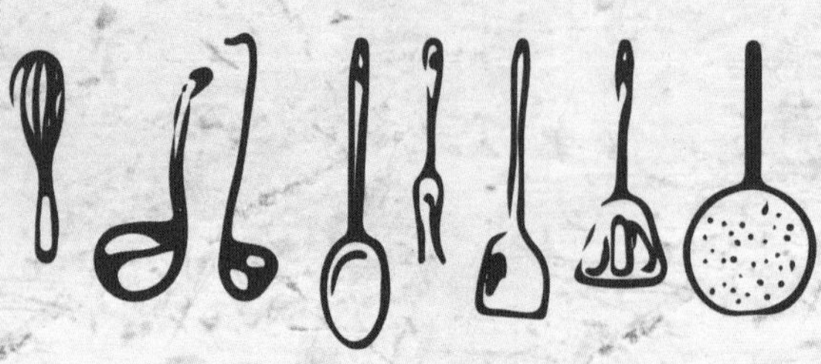